History

The Greatest Empires That Defined Our World

Table of Contents

Introduction

There is so much history to the world. However, in this book we cover the extensive past of three huge and great empires. Those include the Roman Empire, the Persian Empire, and the Mongol Empire. All three had great rises, and then had great falls, one shorter than the other. One was outlived while another is known as the greatest of all empires. Which one is which? Read on to find out and grow your knowledge on the rich past of all three empires.

Chapter 1: The Roman Empire

The Roman Empire's beginning is embroiled in many myths. There are traces that have been found by different archaeologists. This evidence shows evidence of early settlements that began on Palatine Hill and dated all the way back to 750 BC. This evidence also ties in closely to the established statement of Rome beginning founded on April 21, 753 BC. This was traditionally celebrated with the festival of Parilia in Rome. In this chapter, you are going to dive into the rich history of the Roman Empire. From kings to major events, you will find out how the Roman Empire was built up and then how it met its fall.

Roman History Timeline

753 BC	This is the year in which Rome was founded by Romulus and Remus.
753 - 509 BC	This is considered to be the time of the kings.
509 BC	Rome then became a republic by overthrowing the king. (Tarquin the Proud)
494 BC	This is the year of the Revolt of Plebeians against Patricians. Plebeians gave the right to choose tribunes and have a voice inside the government.
458 BC	General Cincinnatus was brought out of retirement and took a position of a dictator in order to save Rome. As soon as he had won the battles, he then returned to Rome. He resigned and went back to his fields.
451 BC	The first law code was developed in Rome. It was called the Twelve Tables.
390 BC	Gauls invaded Rome.
312 BC	The first aqueduct and the first major road was started.
340 - 338 BC	Rome had defeated the Latin League.
275 BC	Rome had control of the Italian peninsula.
264 - 241 BC	This was the years of the first war between Carthage and Rome. It was called the First Punic War.

218 - 201 BC	This was the years of the second war with Carthage. It was called the Second Punic War and is was with Hannibal as the leader in the Carthage army.
202 BC	The Romans defeated Hannibal in the battle of Zama.
200 BC	Concrete was used for the first time in the Roman town called Palestrina.
149 - 146 BC	This was the years of the Third Punic War.
89 BC	The Roman citizenship was then extended to Italian and Latin allies.
85 BC	This year was the year in which the heating system that was known as the hypocaust was used in order to spread heat to most of the public baths.
73 - 71 BC	This was the years of the Slave revolt that was led by Spartacus, a gladiator.
67 BC	The Mediterranean sea was eradicated of pirates by Pompey.
60 BC	Crassus, Pompey, and Julius Caesar formed an alliance that was known as First Triumvirate.
58 - 51 BC	Baul was conquered by Julius Caesar and is known today by the name of France.
55 - 54 BC	Britain was attacked by Julius Caesar.
49 BC	Julius Caesar gave the order to disband the army instead of beginning a civil war.
49 - 45 BC	These were the years of the civil war. Julius Caesar won the war.
44 BC	On March 15th of this year, Julius Caesar was assassinated on the Ides.
44 - 30 BC	A civil war began between Octavian and Marcus Antony
42 BC	The argument that taxes on rich women were unfair. Hortensia was the woman to begin this argument.
31 BC	Cleopatra and Marcus Antony were defeated during the battle of Actium.
30 BC	Cleopatra and Marcus Antony escaped into Egypt. They then committed suicide.
27 BC	Octavian claimed the title of Augustus with the beginning of the Empire age. He assumes all of the power of magistrates inside the Roman government. It began the Pax Romana, which is translated to Peace of Rome.
6 AD	Vigils were developed in order to protect and fight the fires in the city of Rome under the leader Augustus.
19 AD	Pont du Guard aqueduct was built in Gaul. It still stands today in France.

30 AD	Jesus Christ was crucified in Jerusalem.
64 AD	Christians were blamed for starting the Great Fire by Nero. It began the persecution of all Christians.
66 - 73 AD	The Jewish revolt began.
69 - 96 AD	This marked the Flavian period.
79 AD	Vesuvius began to bury the towns of Pompeii and Herculaneum.
80 AD	The Colosseum was finished.
121 - 126 AD	The Hadrian's wall was built in Britain.
130 AD	Hadrian had ordered the building of the Pantheon located in Rome.
96 - 138	The Empire had reached its greatest extent under the Emperors Trajan (96 to 117) and Hadrian (117 to 138).
138 - 193 AD	This was the Antonine Period of the Rulers.
197 AD	The Roman soldiers were given permission to marry while they were on duty.
235 - 285 AD	This was the Time of Anarchy. This was the legitimate emperor for a long time.
293 AD	Diocletian split the empire into four different sections that were ruled by two emperors that ruled together.
303 AD	This is the year that the persecution of the Christians that got very heated.
312 AD	Constantine I had invaded Italy and took over, along with Licinius.
313 AD	Freedom was given to Christians for worship and churches. It was deemed a real religion of the empire by Edict of Milan.
324 AD	Constantine I won over Licinius and then took over the sole rule of the empire.
330 AD	Capitol had moved from Rome to Constantinople by Constantine I. This is now known as Istanbul.
395 AD	The empire was divided into West and East.
410 AD	Rome had lost its control over Britain.
452 AD	Attila the Hun had invaded Italy. This army stayed out of Rome by request of Pope Leo I.
453 AD	Attila the Hun met his demise and died.
455 AD	Rome was sacked by Vandals.

476 AD	This was the Fall of the Western Roman Empire by the invasion of the Goths.
533 - 554 AD	Justinian had begun to recapture the Western Roman Empire.
554 - 1453 AD	The Eastern Empire had survived as the Byzantine Empire.
1453 AD	The Byzantine Empire was defeated by Ottoman Turks.

Early Kings of the Roman Empire

The word "King" was a loaded word for those that lived in the Roman Empire. When this empire began, a king typically ruled city-states. A city-state is a city that has surrounding territories that were big enough to form a state. Other aristocrats of equal power that was around the monarch gave advice, but if necessary would force the king from his throne. They would pick a successor. However kings, due to hereditary were normal.

After dealing with successions of kings, the Romans were fed up with the system and were willing to do something new, they went to the techniques that were used by Greece. It was much like democracy is today. It took a lot of time and battles, but Rome fought against the king in order for a new government. However, here is a list of kings that served with power in the Roman times.

753 - 715 BC: Romulus

Romulus is a legend in his own right. Tatius, the Sabine king of Cures, ruled with Romulus from the time of the raping of the Sabine women, all the way to his death in the year 648 BC. Romulus was the first king of Rome. His story was a typical "rags to riches". His story also included a miraculous birth much like Jesus and the exposure of an infant that was unwanted. In "Britain

Begins" by Barry Cunliffe, he describes the story of Romulus as a story of "love, rape, treachery, and murder".

Romulus had a twin brother named Remus. The founding of Rome is just one of the most familiar legends. The basic legend is of how Romulus first became king and it begins with the god named Mars, which impregnated Rhea Silvia, a Vestal Virgin. Rhea Silvia was the daughter of a deposed king. A Vestal Virgin is a virgin that was consecrated to Vesta and is vowed to chastity and shared in the charge of maintaining the sacred fire that was burning on the altar for the goddess.

Outline of the Legend of Romulus's Birth and Rise

- After the birth of Romulus and Remus, Mar's sons, the king ordered that they be left for death in the Tiber River.
- When the basket holding the twins washed up on shore, a wolf provides milk and a woodpecker that was named Picus feeds the boys.
- Faustulus, a shepherd, find the twin boys and then brings them back to his home.
- After the boys grow up, they restore the throne of Alba Longa to their grandfather, the rightful ruler.
- They then set out in order to found their own city.
- Ultimately there is sibling rivalry, which leads to Romulus slaying his own brother.
- After, Romulus becomes the very first king and the founder of Rome.
- Rome was named after the first king.

That was an outline of the legend of the twin brothers; however, there is evidence of another story in which shows a more realistic approach to the beginning of Rome. You must remember that the first words written on this story were in Latin, and it was roughly translated. So, interpretation played a very large role in stating facts about the twins. Here is some more detail on the matter.

It is thought that the suckling wolf was actually a prostitute that found and cared for the twin boys. If this is true, then the story of the wolf suckling the twins is only interpretation of a word in Latin for brothel cave; lupanar. This word is Latin for both "she-wolf", as well as "brothel"; "lupa".

Archaeologists uncovered the lupercale. This cave was uncovered on Palatine Hill located in Rome. Many think that it was the same cave in which the twin boys sucked by the lupa. So, if you look at the possible facts, it is far more likely that a prostitute found the boys and took care of them, rather than a savage she-wolf that just happened to have milk from her pups still.

Romulus may not have been the founder of Rome. It may have had a different origin. Here are some details on this. The Vestal Virgin, Rhea Silvia, was the mother of Romulus and Remus. She was said to have been the daughter of Numitor and the niece of the king, Amulius of Alba Longa located in Latium.

Alba Longa was the area that was located near the location of Rome. It was about twelve miles southeast; however, the city was yet to be built on the seven hills. A Vestal Virgin was considered to be a special priestly post of the goddess Vesta. It was reserved for women that offered great honor, as well as privilege. It also was a virginal status, as the name implies.

In fear, the king was scared of being challenged by Numitor's descendants, so he tried to prevent the birth of any heirs by forcing his niece to become a Vestal. This would force her to remain a virgin and never giving birth to someone who could challenge him for the throne. Smart plan, or so he had thought. Amulius thought wrong, evidently.

The penalty for violating chastity for a Vestal was a cruel death. Rhea Silvia had survived the violation of the vow long enough to give birth to her twins, Romulus and Remus. Unfortunately for her, just like later Vestal Virgins who ended up violating the vow, she was buried alive. It is important to note here that Vestals were also used as scapegoats when the luck of Rome seemed to be teetering. The Vestal was blamed for breaking the vow and bringing down bad luck on Rome, and then being buried alive.

Romulus and Remus Run-Down

King Numitor of ALba Longa was ejected from the throne by his younger brother by the name of Amulius. In order to do away with any possible pretended to take away the throne, Amulius had murdered the sones of Numitor and forced his daughter, Rhea Silvia, to become a Vestal. However, Mars, the god of war was so enchanted by Rhea Silvia's beauty. He had his way with her while she slept. In result, Rhea Silvia had twins by the name Romulus and Remus. Amulius was enraged by this and threw Rhea Silvia thrown into the Tiber river. (All though some say that she was buried alive.) She was caught under the waves by the river god and married her.

The twin boys were set adrift on the river inside of a reed basket. The boys floated downstream until the basket was caught in some branches of a fig tree. This is where they were found by a wolf who gave them milk. They were then found by a shepherd. Another version of the founding story tells that the shepherd found them and took them to his wife who had just lost a baby due to being stillborn. She still had milk, so she nursed the boys. It was said that the shepherd's wife had been a prostitute before their marriage. Which of the stories is the original is pretty hard to tell.

The twins grew up with the shepherd and his wife. The couple told the twins of their original origin. The boys built an army and marched on Alba Longa. Amulius was killed in battle, and Numitor was then restored to the throne. The twins had decided to found a city that was close to where they had washed up and raised. The twins fought on which hill to found as the city. Romulus favored the Palatine, whereas, Remus chose another, it could possibly have been Aventine.

Aeneas Founding Story

Although the story of Romulus and Remus is a very popular one, there is another story of the founding of Rome. The tale of Aeneas was more popular during the times of Rome. Aeneas was said to have been a hero that fought the Greeks in the Trojan wars. Aeneas was the son of Venus and was a mortal father, he had escaped as the city of Troy was tore down. After he landed in Latium from traveling on the Tiber river. Aeneas had married the daughter of King Latinus, which angered King Turnus of Rutili, who had his eye on her as well. They engaged in war over this princess. Of course, the son of Venus, Aeneas had his victory.

The fall of Troy is dated to be around 1220 BC. In order to fill the years from Aeneas up to Romulus, the Romans were required to create a string of fictional Kings in order to make the tale work. This was done across all of the generations with some ease from Ascanius, which was the son of Aeneas to Numitor, the grandfather of Romulus and Remus.

The Latin's settled in the wider part of Rome around the year 1,000 BC. Though early settlements were not mistaken for anything like the city. They herded sheep, cattle, goats, and kept sheep. They lived in huts and lived in a primitive way. The rise of the city of Rome was never a certainty, but it had advantages right from the beginning. Rome lies only a few short miles from the sea and with the possibilities of trade, there was definite potential. It was central to the Italian peninsula, which lies central to the entire Mediterranean Sea. Italy is kept guarded by the Alps from the North and by the sea all around. Add this to the influence of the Greeks, which were settling just south of Italy. They founded cities like Tarentum and Cumea, which brought the advancement of the civilization into the county. The Romans learned fundamental skills like reading and writing from the Greeks. Even the religion is derived from Greek mythology, like Zeus, Area, etc.

The Roman Army Structure

The Roman army was broken into different groups. This was to ensure a clear chain of command while in battle. The smallest of units were called the contubernium, which was made up of a group of eight soldiers. These men then marched together and shared a specific tent or a room located at the fort. Ten contubernium was made up of a century, which typically was made of eighty men. They were commanded by a centurion. Six centuries would then be combined in order to make up a cohort.

The ten Cohorts would be put together in order to make up a legion, which is about six thousand men. The first cohort of the legion was normally twice the size of a typical cohort and had the best of soldiers. The legion was man of infantry. It was also the backbone of the army. Each of the legions contained four lines or group. The front line soldiers were the velites, who were trained to throw the spears at the enemy side. Behind these soldiers were the hastatus and preinceps. These soldiers did most of the battle fighting. They had swords and light armour. The last line were the triarius, who wore the heavy armour. In addition to the legionnaires, the auxiliary cohorts of the cavalry were the archers.

Marriage in Rome

Many of the marriages in Rome were arranged by the couple's parents. The popular month for the marriages was in June. The girl would often times be the age of thirteen while the boy of in the marriage would be a couple years older than her. The bride would take the childhood toys and the clothing, then offer them to the goddess Venus or to the household gods that were called lares and penates. A pid would then be sacrificed on the day of the marriage and prayers would be made to Juno. The father of the bride would sign a document of the marriage and gifts from the family of the bride would be given the family of the groom. The wedding day would end with the groom pretending that he was taking the bride away from the mother for the remembrance of the legendary story of Sabian women that were in early Rome.

Women and the Roman Society

Women in this society were given very little power. Politics, as well as trades, were dominated by men. The Romans often feared the women with power like queens. For example, the Romans did not favor Cleopatra in fear that Julius Caesar was under a spell put on him by this foreign queen. Another woman, Queen Boudicca, lead a revolt against Britain. Yet there were many times in which women influenced the process of politics. Following the assassination of the leader Julius Caesar, the political leaders then targeted approximately 1,400 rich women in order to raise the taxes for the war. Hortensia, the daughter of a great lawyer, spoke out against this and caused the political rulers to tax only 400 of these women.

The lives of the women varied based on the position that they held in society. The women who came from the wealthy level had much of their daily labor done by the slaves. A slave would aid in washing the female master's face, give her a massage with oils, and spend hours upon hours setting her hair into beautiful curls. The wealthy women would spend a lot of their days just socializing and planning their next event to entertain their friends.

Few women were lucky enough to lead a leisurely life. Women were in charge of bringing up the children and keeping the house running. Since there was no birth control available in Roman times, women were most times pregnant. Men would leave the home in the morning to work until approximately noon, and then they would spend the afternoon relaxing at the bath or a public event to be entertained. When a man would return home, he would expect to find the home in order.

Women had to wash the clothes by hand weekly. Clothes were washed in a large sized tub with a soap called lye. They would be laid on the bushes or the ground to be dried by the sun and the wind. Large sized blankets would be taken to a local stream while the smaller items were washed inside of a bowl at home in the kitchen. The richer of women would have their slaves to the work or they would take their clothing to a washing store.

The lower class women would keep the home clean. They would clean the home using a twig broom and brushes that were made from animal hairs. Oil and Fire for lamps were the responsibility of the women, as well as keeping the fuel for the fire in the colder months. Going shopping for food and other home essentials were also a daily task for many of the Roman women. On top of these specific responsibilities, the women were also in charge of spinning the yarn and making clothing for their entire family by hand.

Many of the women also worked in the areas outside of the home. In the countryside, men were in charge of working the harvest in the fields. Women were put in charge of making the cheese, pickling foods, and washing the wool. In the cities, women worked in the shops with their

13

craftsman husband and helped run the store. There were a great number of women entertainers, though it was not a highly thought of position in society. There is even evidence that women may have been gladiators at a different time in society.

Roman Children

In the early days of the city of Rome, the father would decide whether a child would live or if they would die. If the father decided, the child would be abandoned to die. When a child was eight or nine days old, the father would choose a name for the baby. Three names would be given to a male. The child's first name was a personal one, the second was that of the clan, and the third name was a name from the family. Girls were only given one. However, later a second name was added, which was a family name.

Roman Schools

Schools were formed in an area of the town. There were many children that attended for only five years in order to earn a basic form of education. Students used the wax tablets to write on and an abacus in order to do math. Discipline was extremely strict, and the teacher would have full authority to beat the children if they did not pay attention.

Some of the children went to secondary school that was known as a grammaticus. There they would learn geometry, history, and astronomy. Those who wanted to continue the education would learn the art of rhetoric or discussion, in which they would use it in political debates. Those who were wealthy would send their children over to Athens, the pinnacle of the education in this time. Athens developed a very strong reputation for education from the time of Socrates.

Roman Food

Italians are known for pasta and pizza, but they were not a part of the typical diet in Rome. In early Rome, food was made up of mostly soups and boiled meats. They did not even have baked bread. Later with the influence of different cultures that they had conquered, The Romans then adapted different recipes into their menu. The rich had a very large variety, as well as quantity of foods to eat. Breakfast would consist of bread and cheeses. Lunch would offer bread, meat, as well as fruit. Then dinner, which would be served in the late afternoon would be a three course meal. The Plebeians did not have a large variety or even a good quantity of food. Meat would be served only on special occasion, but it was not a typically part of their diets.

Preparation of the Roman food would take a lot of work. Flour was ground between two different heavy stones and then would be sifted. Pestles and mortars, seen as a symbol for pharmacists today, would be utilised in order to crush up nuts and herbs. Most Romans loved their foods spicy with lots of pepper included. Utensils were made of iron and were extremely expensive, so the average person would use bronze knives and bronze spoons. Forks were not used by Romans, who often just ate with their hands. Plates for the average person were made of pottery or wood while the richer ate off of metal plates made of tin, pewter, or bronze. Romans did not use soap to clean the plates and eating utensils. They just rinsed them in water. Metal dishes were cleaned by rubbing sand on them, and then rinsing them in water.

Battles that Helped Shape Rome

The Ancient Romans stood and fought many battles and wars in order to expand, as well as protect their empire. There were also different civil wars in which Romans fought Romans to gain power. Here are the major battles and wars that were fought by the Romans.

The Punic Wars were fought between Carthage and Rome from the years 264 BC all the way to 146 BC. Carthage was a very large city that was located on the coast of the continent North Africa. This sounds like a very long way away, but Carthage was just a short voyage by sea from Rome just across the Mediterranean Sea. Both of the cities were major powers at this time, and both were wanting to expand the empires. Ads they grew, they began to clash and then soon war broke out. There were three parts of the Punic wars, and they were fought over a course of over 100 years.

- First Punic War: This war was fought in the years of 264 to 241 BC. It was fought largely over the island of Sicily. This meant that there were a lot of fighting on the sea where Carthage had the advantage with a larger navy than Rome. However, Rome had quickly built up a navy that included over 100 ships. Rome also invented the Corvus, which is a type of assault bridge that had allowed the soldiers to board the enemy vessels. Rome soon then dominated the Carthage and won this war.

- Second Punic War: This was fought over the years of 218 to 201 BC. Carthage had more success in this fight against the Roman legions. The Carthage leader and the general, Hannibal had made a dangerous crossing over the Alps in order to attack Rome and the northern part of Italy. This crossing was made famous due to the fact that he had also brought a large number of elephants with him. Hannibal was a smart general and had won many battles against the Romans. However, despite the 16 years of fighting, Hannibal was not able to conquer the huge city of Rome. Once Rome counterattacked Carthage, Hannibal was then forced to retreat. The final battle in this specific war was the Battle of Zama in which the Roman general, Scipio Africanus, had defeated Hannibal.

- Third Punic War: This war was fought in the years of 149 to 146 BC. In this war, the Romans were attacked in the city of Carthage. After three years of laying siege to this city, the Roman army had broken through the walls and then burned it down.

Battle of Cynoscephalae

This battle took place in the year 364 VC. In this specific battle, the Roman Legion was under the rule of Titus Flaminius, and they defeated Macedonian Army that was led by Philip V. This certain battle was extremely important due to the successors of the Greek leader, Alexander the Great.

Third Servile War

This war was fought in the years 73 to 71 BC. It began when 78 gladiators, which included the leader Spartacus, had escaped and then began a rebellion. Soon they had more than 120,000 slaves and other traveler's join them to invade the countryside. They successfully fought back Roman soldiers until eight legions were dispatched in order to destroy them. The fighting was long and drawn out, but eventually, Spartacus was defeated.

Caesar's Civil War

This civil war was fought in the years 49 to 45 BC. It was also called the Great Roman Civil War. The legions of Julius Caesar fought against the legions that were supported by the Senate of Pompey the Great. The war lasted four years until finally Caesar defeated Pompey and then became the Dictator of Rome. This then signaled the end of the Roman Republic. The famous moment of this war was when Caesar had crossed the Rubicon River. This meant that he was going to war against the city of Rome. Today the term "crossing the Rubicon" is used to say that a person had reached the point of no return and now cannot go back.

Battle of Actium

This was in the year 31 BC. In this specific battle, Octavian forces were led by Marcus Agrippa. They defeated combined forces of the Roman general Marc Antony, as well as the Egyptian Pharaoh Cleopatra VII. In result, Octavian then became the power of Rome and would then become Rome's first Emperor. He would then change his name to Augustus. Little fun fact; the month of August is named after Augustus.

Chapter 2: The Persian Empire

Just like the Roman Empire, the Persian Empire has a long and rich history. In this chapter, we are going to dive into this rich history. The Persian Empire included what is now Iran. In fact, the name Persia was the name of Iran up to the year of 1935. The height of this empire was approximately 500 BS. The Achaemenids were the founding dynasty of the empire. It had conquered Asia as far at Greece, the Indus River, and North Africa. It also included what is now Libya and Egypt.

The start of the Persian empire is set at different times that are stated by different scholars. However, the real force behind this expansion was due to Cyrus II, also known as Cyrus the Great in the mid-sixth century BC. Cyrus was a part of Achaemenid Empire. The first capital was Hamadan and then moved to Pasargadae. In the year 330 BC, Macedonian Greeks were led by Alexander the Great. They overthrew the Achaemenids and then established the Seleucid Empire. The Seleucids were then followed by the Parthian and the Sassanid dynasties. The Sassanids were then defeated by Arab caliphs in the mid-seventh century AD, and by the year 651, the Persian Empire had been finished.

The Persian Empire Timeline

550 BC	Cyrus rules. Cyrus II, later known as Cyrus the Great, comes into power as the king of Ashan in the western Persis. Under the control of Cyrus, all of Persis is then united. He begins the Achaemenid dynasty.
550 BC	Cyrus gets attacked. King Astyages of Media attacks the leader Cyrus. During this fight, some of the Astyages men turn on the leader and Cyrus then becomes the victor in this war. He goes on to conquer Lydia by defeating the Medes.
539 BC	Cyrus captured Babylon. Cyrus continues on his con quest and soon he takes Babylon under his control.

536 BC	Two hundred years before the conquering of Babylon, the prophet Isaiah had written of the great ruler by the name Cyrus who will allow the Jews to rebuild their temple. When the scroll is read found and read to Cyrus, he then commands that the captive Jews in Babylon be allowed to return to their holy city.
533 - 529 BC	Cyrus continues to take over even more lands. In the year 533 BC, he invaded India. He then later dies in this battle in the year 529 BC.
529 - 522 BC	After the death of Cyrus, his son, Cambyses II then goes into rule. He conquers Egypt and Cyprus, which extended the empire more. He dies in the year 522 BC.
521 BC	Darius claims his throne, but Bardiya, Cambyses' brother, claims the throne as well. Bardiya is then eventually defeated and then Darius then becomes the king of Persia.
521 BC	Darius divided the empire into provinces that are called satrapies, which is governed by a satrap. He then linked the empire by roads and a common currency. He also allowed the Jews to continue reguilding the temple after disputes from neighbor areas.
499 BC	Lydia joins Persia after the conquering by Cyrus in 546 BC, but they then rebel in the year 499 BC. Darius put down the rebellion.
490 - 479 BC	The Greeks and the Persians battle for territory for many years. At times, the Persians won, and other times the Greeks won. In the year 485 BC, Darius died.
485 - 465 BC	Xerxes I comes into power after the death of the leader Darius. He then continues the war on Greece. The Persians burn Athens to the ground in the year 480 BC but are then defeated at Salamis in the following year once the fleet is sunk. Xerxes is then assassinated in the year 465 BC.
465 - 424 BC	The son of Xerxes, Artaxerxes, takes over the empire. During his time of power he allows the cupbearer, nehemiah, to return to Jerusalem in order to restore the walls to protect this city. In the year 447 BC, a satrap from Syria rises against this.
404 - 359 BC	Artaxerxes takes the throne in the year 404 BC after the reign of Darius II. He then rules longer than other Persian kings. During this time, Egypt revolts successfully.
359 - 338 BC	Egypt does not stay independent for long. In the year 343 BC, Persian then regains its control. Artaxerxes III is then assassinated in the year 338 BC. Arses takes over; however, is then assassinated just two years later.

336 - 330 BC	Darius III ends up taking over. In the year 334 BC, Alexander the Great of Macedonia then invades Central Asia. Darius loses three of the battles with Alexander and then defeated in the year 331 BC. he is murdered in the year 330 BC. The great Persian Empire is then conquered and finished. It began with a conquest and the ended in defeat. However, it will always be remembered as a very powerful force that swept through Asia, Africa, along with Europe.

Achaemenid Empire 550 to 330 BC

The Achaemenids were the ruling dynasty of the leader Cyrus the Great and his family from 550 to 330 BC when it was then conquered by Alexander the Great. Cyrus's empire included Ethiopia, Libya, Thrace, Afghanistan, Macedonia, and the Punjab, along with everything in between.

Achaemenid List of Kings

- Cambyses I
- Cyrus II: 550 - 530 BC
- Cambyses II: 530 - 522 BC
- Bardiya: 522 BC
- Darius I: 522 - 486 BC
- Xerxes I: 486 - 465 BC
- Artaxerxes I: 465 - 424 BC
- Xerxes II: 424 - 423 BC
- Darius II (Ochus): 423 - 404 BC
- Artaxerxes II (Arsaces): 404 - 359 BC
- Artaxerxes III (Ochus): 359 - 338 BC
- Artaxerxes IV (Arses): 338 - 336 BC
- Darius III: 336 - 330 BC

The vast region was conquered by Cyrus; however, his descendants were not able to be controlled from the king's palace located in Persepolis or in Pasargadae. Therefore, each region ended up having a regional governor or a satrap.

Architectural styles that were common through Achaemenid included distinctive columned buildings that were called apadanas, extensive rock carvings, as well as stone reliefs, climbing staircases, and the first version of the Persian Garden, which was divided into four parts. Luxury items that identified in this time were jewellery that was made with polychrome inlay, animal head bracelets, as well as carinated bowls of silver and gold.

Royal Road

The Royal Road of Achaemenids was a very big intercontinental deal that was built by king Darius the Great in order to allow access to the cities that were conquered by the Persian empire. It also was the same road that Alexander the Great had used in order to conquer the Achaemenid dynasty a century and a half later on.

The Royal Road had led from the Aegean Sea into Iran. It ran the length of 1,500 miles. A major branch connected the cities of Kirkuk, Susa, Nineveh, Hattusa, Edessa, and Sardis. The venture from Susa to Sardis as reported to have taken at least 90 days when on foot, and three more in order to get to the Mediterranean coast. The venture would have been a lot faster on horseback, and carefully placed stations for travelers. From Susa, the road had connected to Persepolis and India. It intersected with the other roads that lead into the ancient allied and competing kingdoms of Baktria, Media, and Sogdiana.

Architectural feature of the Royal Road is a bit difficult since the road was built following the older roads. The sections that were in tact during Darius's time, like that by Gordion and Sardis, were constructed with a cobble pavement on top of a low embankment from 5 to 7 meters in width, and in some placed it faced with a curb of dressing stone.

There were 111 way posting stations the were reported to have existed on the main branch of the road between Sardis and Susa, where there were fresh horses to keep the traveler's going. There were a handful of way stations that were identified archaeologically. One of the possible way stations is as large as 40 X 30 meters and had five rooms. It was near the site of Kuh-e Qale. Another site is located by JinJan, located in Iran.

Much of what we know today about the Royal Road comes from Herodotus, which was a Greek historian who describes the postal system. Archaeological evidence offers suggestions that there were several precursors to the road. It states that a portion of the road connects to Gordion on the coast and was likely used by Cyrus during his conquest of Anatolia. It is quite possible that the first roads were established in the tenth century BC. These roads were used as trade routes by the Hittites and the Assyrians at Boghakzoy.

Later on, Roman roads were constructed along Persian roads. Some of the Roman roads are still used today, meaning that there are parts of the Royal Road have been used for over 3,000 years. It is also argued that a southern route that lays across the Euphrates at Zeugma and across the Cappodocia, ending at Sardis, was the main part of the Royal Road. This was a route that was taken by Cyrus in the younger part of 401 BC. It is possible that Alexander the Great traveled this route while conquering a large part of Eurasia in the fourth century.

The northern part of the route was proposed by many scholars as the main part of three possible routes through Ankara located in Turkey and into Armenia, which crossed the Euphrates in the hills close to the Keban dam. All of the segments were used before and after the Achaemenids.

23

Achaemenid Languages

Due to the Achaemenid empire being so extensive, there were many languages that were required for administration purposes. Several of the inscriptions that were found, like the Behistun Inscription, were translated into many different languages.

The primary languages that were used by the Achaemenids included Old Persian in which the ruler spoke, Elamite in which was spoken by the original people of Iraq, and Akkadian in which was the ancient language of the Assyrians, as well as the Babylonians. Old Persian had its own script, which was developed by the Achaemenid rulers and was passed on cuneiform edges while the Elamite and the Akkadian languages were typically written in cuneiform. Egyptian inscriptions are known to be a lesser level, and one translation of the Behistun inscription was found in Aramaic.

Seleucid Empire 330 to 170 BC

Preceding the death of Alexander the Great, his empire was cut into many different satrapies. One of these were the Seleucid Empire, it was based in Babylon and headed by Seleucus, which was also known as Nicator. While the Seleucid empire was pretty successful, and continuing to get most of Alexander's empire, the Seleucids ended up succumbing to the Roman empire in the first century BC.

This empire began when Selecucos I, which was one of Alexander the Great's past favourite companions. He was given the satrapy of Babylon in the second division of this empire in the year 321 BC. He first ruled it very briefly until the year 315 BC, when he was forced to flee into Egypt under the pressure of Antigonos. While there, he prepared his revenge with aid from Ptolemy and then succeeded to take it back after the battle of Gaza in the year 305 BC. He also then inherited the Asian part of Antigonos' empire after its fall in the battle of Ipsos in the year

301 BC. Having secured the kingdom's eastern part, Seleucos had managed to conquer most of Alexander's empire, defeating the Demetrios and Lysimachos. He was then murdered in the year 281 BC on the eve of his success by a man he had supported for the Egyptian throne. His name was Ptolemy Keraunos.

After Seleucos died, things then became worse for his successors. During the reigns of Antiochos I, Antiochos II, Seleucos II, as well as Seleucos III, the empire had struggled due to the rebellions of Pergammum, Bythinia, Bactria, along with Parthia. Internal struggles began during this time, which also continued until the end of the empire. The Seleucids also fought the Galatians who had devastated Anatolia, and also was against the rebellious elements.

Antiochos III was only eighteen years old in the year of 223 BC when he inherited this disorganized empire. Over the following 25 years, he fought down most of the rebellious states with a great tour. He made his difficult retreat in the east successfully while fighting the Bactrians and Parthians. It made a very profitable treaty with the Indian ruler by the name Sophagasenos, and it confirmed his superiority on the rebellious side. He also made an expedition East Arabian in the year 204 BC. He defeated the Ptolemies two time, which allowed him to gain control of Koile Syria near the year 198 BC.

Antiochos III also led a war against the Rome Empire in the wake of the expansion in Anatolia. Despite the advice of Carthaginian Hannibal Barca, he decided not to follow it. He was then defeated in the battle of Magnesia ad Sipylum in the year 190 BC. The consequences of this treaty and the kingdom was ruined shortly after. He died in the year 187 BC during a campaign.

The Parthian Empire was also known as the Arsacid Empire. It was the most enduring of the empires. After the Parni nomads had settled in Parthia and built a small independent kingdom, they then rose to power under the lead of king Mithradates the Great. The Parthian empire occupied all of the modern areas of Iraq, Iran, and Armenia. It also included part of Turkey, Azerbaijan, Georgia, Turkmenistan, Tajikistan, and Afghanistan. For brief periods, it also included territories in Pakistan, Lebanon, Syria, Israel, as well as Palestine. At the end of this loosely organized empire, the king was defeated in the year 224 BC.

After the fall of the empire Achaemenid, Parthian as then governed by the Seleucid kings, which was a Macedonian dynasty that had ruled in the Asian territories that were formerly Persian Empire. In the year 245 BC, a satrap by the name of Andragoras had revolted from the Seleucid king Seleucus II, who had succeeded to the throne. In the year 238 BC, they had occupied the district that was known as Astavene. Three years after, a Parnian leader by the name of Tiridates had ventured further south and then seized the rest of Parthia. There was a counter offensive move made by king Seleucus that ended in disaster. Hyrcania was then subdued by the Parni. Arsaces I was the brother of Tiridate and was the first king of the Parthians. The capital was located in Hecatompylos.

The kings Arsaces I and II, Phriapathus, Phraates I had recognized the Seleucid king as their superior. This was especially after the campaign of Antiochus III, who had reconquered the lost territories in the east between the years 209 to 204 BC. The Arsacid dynasty was then recognized as the lawful ruler; however, the kings had to pay tribute.

After the year 188 BC, once Antiochus died, a new phase of the Parthian expansion had begun. King Mithradates I the Great first attacked the kingdom of Bactria. He covered his rear, moved to the west, and he conquered Media, which was one of the most crucial parts of the empire of Seleucid. In the month of July of the year 141 BC, Mithradates had captured the Seleucid capital. Then in October, he had reached Uruk in the south part of Babylonia. His enemy, Demetrius II, had tried to conquer his territories back, but was defeated and then was caught. Two years later, Elam was an addition to the Parthian empire.

Parthian Dynasty Government

After the conquest of Assyria, Media, Elam, and Babylonia, the Parthians was forced to organize their empire. The elite of the countries was the Greek, and the new rulers were forced to adapt to the customs. Cities retained their ancient rights, and the civil administration had remained undisturbed. Legends were written using the Greek alphabet, and this was a practice that continued all the way into the second century when the knowledge of the language declined.

Another great source of inspiration was the Achaemenid dynasty that once ruled the Persian Empire. Courtiers spoke Persian and also used the Pahlavi script. The Royal court had traveled from capital to capital in order to teach this. They were led by Cyrus the Great. The Parthian monarch was the ruler of his own empire, as well as approximately eighteen vassal kings.

The empire was not centralized. There were many different languages, and there were many cultures and many economic systems that made this empire up. However, the loose ties between the parts were the key to the survival of the empire. In the second century, the most important capital by the name of Ctesiphon, as then captured more than three different times by the Romans. The empire survived anyways, this is because there were other centers in the empire. On the other hand, the fact this empire was a conglomerate of kingdoms, provinces, and marks, and the city-states could at times weaken the state of Parthian. This explains why the expansion came to an end once the conquest of Mesopotamia and Iran happened.

Local potentates had played a crucial role, and the king was forced to respect their privileges. There were several noble families that had a vote in the Royal council. The Suren clan even had the right to crown the Parthian king. Every aristocrat was expected to retain an army all of his own. When the throne was held by a weak ruler, the divisions among the nobility would become very dangerous.

The constituent parts of this empire were surprisingly independent. For example, they were allowed to make their own coinage. As long as the local elite had paid tribute, the Parthian kings never interfered. The system worked well. Towns like Ctesiphon, Ecbatan, Seleucia, Rhagae, Nisa, Hecatompylos, and Susa had thrived. Tribute was one of the royal incomes, another was tolls. Parthia had controlled the Silk Road and the route from Mediterranean Sea all the way to China.

Western Wars

The Seleucid empire had attacked from two sides, the Parthians attacked from the east side, and the Romans attacked from the west. In the year 69 BC, the two enemies concluded in a treaty. The Euphrates would become a border. Six years after, the Roman commander by the name Pompey the Great had conquered what was left of the empire.

In the year 53 BC, Crassus, a Roman general had invaded Parthia. At Carrhae or Harran; however, he was defeated by the Parthian commander Surena. He was a member of the Suren clan. The was the start of a series of wars that lasted for three centuries.

The Parthian armies were made of two different types of cavalry. They were heavy armed and armoured cataphracts. It also consisted of light brigades of mounted archers. The Parthians were hard to defeat by the Romans due to their reliance on heavy infantry. However, the Parthians could not occupy conquered countries, they were too unskilled with siege warfare.

Sassanid Dynasty 226 to 651 AD

This empire is also called the Sasanian Empire. The Sasanian dynasty was established by Ardashir I after defeating the Arsacid king, Artabanus IV and had ended when the king Yazdegerd III lost in a fourteen year struggle to drive out the Arabs from his Empire.

The empire's territory was made up of areas that are known today by Iraq, Iran, Arran, Armenia, Turkmenistan, Georgia, Uzbekistan Tajikistan, UAE, Afghanistan, Oman, Yemen, Kuwait, Bahrain and eastern parts of Turkey and Syria, as well as Pakistan.

The Sasanian dynasty era is considered to be one of the most crucial and influential periods in the history of Iran. In many ways, this era witnessed the highest of achievement of Iranian civilization and constitutes the last great Iranian Empire before the Muslim conquest and the adoption of Islam. Sasanian Iran had influenced Roman civilization in a large way. Their cultural influence extended far beyond the territorial border, they also played a large role in the formation of medieval art. This influence was carried forward into the early world of Islamic culture. The dynastic empire's unique and aristocratic culture helps transform the Islamic conquest of Iran in the Renaissance period. Much of what is later known as Islamic art, culture, architecture, writing, and many other skills. They were taken mainly from the Iranians into the broader world of the Muslims.

History of the Sasanian Dynasty

The Sasanian Dynasty was began by Ardashir I, which was a descendant of the line of priests of the goddess Anahita at Istakhar. They were located in the Fars province, who actually began during the third century and acquired the governorship of Persis as a vassal king.

His father's name was Papag. He was originally the ruler of a small town that is known today as Khair. But he had managed to depose Gocihr in the year of 205. Gocihr was the last of the vassal kings of the Bazrangids, and he had appointed himself as the ruler. His mother, Rodhagh, was the daughter of a governor in Peris. The eponymous founder of this line was Ardashir I's grandfather, Sasan, which was the great priest of the Temple of Anahita.

Persian Garden

The Persian garden located at Pasargadae was a very large, and formal garden that had stone water channels, as well as orchards. It was built during the ruling of the Achaemenid dynasty of the Persian empire by the name of Cyrus the Great. The Pasargadae garden was one of the earliest built gardens for which there is evidence. It is located and laid out as a lush walled garden in the countryside. It is believed to represent the Judeo and Islamic-Christian ideals of paradise right on earth.

There was archaeological evidence found in the 1970s to the placement of the garden. The palaces were built to provide private access to the gardens. Channels, pavilions, orchards, terraces, pools, walkways, and the enclosing walls characterized the garden, which was laid out in a symmetrically four part system. The fourfold garden was thought to have symbolized the Achaemenid universe of four quarters that were divided by four rivers. There was a central pool inside the garden that led off into the channel into four separate directions.

History reports that the period of the Persian gardens were in many Achaemenid dynasty capitals that included Persepolis and Susa located in Iran, plus many more. The gardens were described as offering a large array of exotic animals, as well as exotic plants that were used for perfumes and medicines like tamarisk, roses, oleander, and violets.

Other Mediterranean cultures that were in contact with the Achaemenid soon after adopted the garden idea. The Pasargadae Garden and other similar gardens in other Achaemenid dynasty cities were believed to be modelled for the gardens of the paradise from the Islamic and the Judeo-Christian beliefs. The word for the enclosure is pairidaeza and is the basis for the word paradise. The gardens were believed to have been the pattern designed from the celestial garden that is described in Koran, and is the model for the Garden of Eden in the bible.

One of the most ancient world's seven wonders is the Hanging Gardens of Babylon. There is archaeological evidence that is yet to be found. However, there is a lush garden that is dated by to 700 BC and is represented on the walls of the Assyrian palace of Sennacherib at Nineveh close to the modern city of Mosul located in Iraq. It was constructed a with a vast water control system in order to support irrigation and fresh water for the city. It was also perhaps used to water the garden.

Chapter 3: The Mongol Empire

Some exclaim that there is no other empire in history that had risen so spectacularly as that of this specific empire. In less than eighty years, a band of warriors had originally comprised of many men grew into an empire that then encompassed all from the Pacific Ocean all the way to the Danube River. This is a story that is about one of the most dramatic series of conquests in history and how it was the Mongols that shattered their invincibility.

Mongol Empire Timeline

450 BC	Turkic speakingtives end up migrating from SIberia to the north of the Aral and Balkash lakes where they would give rise to the Hunds.
250 BC	Chia repels the invasion by the turkic speaking Hsiung-nu.
220 BC	The Hsiung-nu defeated the Yuezhi, who are then forced to move south towards India and Iran.
209 BC	This is the first Hun state.
200 BC	The Hsiung-nu conquer the northern and the western parts of CHina.
48 AD	The Chinese drove Hsiung-nu from China.
50 AD	The Xianbei, which were mounted archers, invaded northern China.
350 AD	The Chinese repelled the invasion by the Ruruan, who in turn then drove the Hsiung-nu west towards the Ural mountains and the Caspian Sea.
350 AD	The turkic speaking Huns then moved western towards Europe. They settled in the plains between Ural and Carpathian mountains.

450 AD	The mongolian empire controlled the territories from Manchuria all the way to the lake Balkas.
451 AD	Attila invaded the Roman Empire.
552 AD	The turkic speaking khanate of Kok or Boumin defeated the Mongols and had extended the empire from Manchuria to the Aral sea.
580 AD	Tardu unifies with the Turks.
601 AD	The Turks siege China's capital Xian under the command of Tardu.
629 AD	The Chinese Tang began an anti-Turk campaign.
651 AD	The Tang annex the Western part of Khanate.
686 AD	The mongolian Kitan raid China.
744 AD	The Chinese Tang dismantle the empire of the Turks.
744 AD	The turkic speaking Uigursconquer the Eastern part of Khanate and expanded from Lake Balkash all the way to the Lake Baykal with the capital in Kara-Balgasun. This is also when the first turkic alphabet was created.
745 AD	The turkic speaking Uigur empire was established in Mongolia.
846 AD	The Kirghiz drove the Uighurs to the west towards the Tarim Basin.
925 AD	The mongolian Kitan expanded towards the eastern part of Mongolia, which drove away the kyrgiz. The Liao dynasty was established.
1100 AD	The turkic speaking Seldjuks expanded into Persia, Mesopotamia, as well as Turkey.
1115 AD	The Jurchen overran the Kitan and established the Karakitai state.
1124 AD	Yeh-lu Ta-Shih led to the remnants of the Kitan army in order to establish the Kara Khitai dynasty.

1130 AD	The Kitan were driven to the southwest, they defeated the Seljuk, and then established the Kara Kitai state.
1135 AD	Mongols were led by Kabul Khan to raid the northern part of China.
1141 AD	The Kara Kitai defeated the Seljuqs at the battle of Qatwan and then destroyed Seljuq power in the Central part of Asia.
1190 AD	Temujin became the king of the Mongols.
1206 AD	Temujin unified all of the mongols and the tatar tribes.
1210 AD	Temujin conquered the kingdom of Xi Xia.
1215 AD	Temujin conquered the kingdom of the Hin Jurchen.
1218 AD	The Mongols conquered the kingdom of Kara Khitai.
1219 AD	Temujin conquered the Khwarizm empire of Ali ad-Din Muhammad.
1220 AD	The Mongols conquered merv.
1221 AD	The Mongols conquered Herat, while on an expedition led by Subedei and Jebe's venture into the west of Caucasus and Russia. They were signing a peace treaty with Venice.
1223 AD	Jebe and Subedei's western Mongol expedition defeated a coalition of Russian princes on the river of Kalka and then the Bulgars. But then they retreated.
1224 AD	Genghis Khan splits the empire into khanates that was ruled by his four sons Ogedei, Jochi, Chaghatay, and Tolui.
1225 AD	Jochidies, and his son named Batu inherited his khanate and then assigned the eastern part to his brother named Orda.
1226 AD	The Jurchen invded northern China dn Korea.
1226 AD	Genghis Khan attacked the Soong state.

1227 AD	Genghis Khan dies and is then succeeded by Ogedei, who ruled over Chaghatay's khanate in the western part of Turkestan, To Liu's Eastern Mongolia, Batu's Blue Horde, and Turkmenistan.
1231 AD	The Mongols invaded korea.
1235 AD	Ogedei moved he Mongol capital to Karakorum.
1237 AD	The Mongols destroyed the northern part of the BUlgars and then invaded Russia under the command of Batu and Subedei.
1238 AD	The Mongols took Vladimir under the command of Batu and Subedei.
1240 AD	Batu's Mongols take Kiev and Chernigov.
1241 AD	Batu's Mongols raided Hungary but then were repelled.
1241 AD	Mongols defeated a joint army of Henry of Slesia and Teutonic Knights at the battle of Liegnitz/Wahlstatt under the command of Chagatai's son Baidar and Ogedei's son.
1241 AD	Ogedei put Baiju in charge of the expansion of Persia.
1241 AD	Ogedei dies, the Mongols then retreat from Europe and Ogedei's widow Toregana takes over.
1241 AD	Batu's younger brother Shayban raided Hungary and then spits it up. Shaybanid Horde was established.
1242 AD	Batu Established a capital in Sarai on the VOlga.
1246 AD	The papal envoy Giovanni da Pian del Carpine to bring a message to the chief of the Mongols.
1246 AD	Kuyuk put general Eliji Fidei in charge of the campaign in order to replace Baiju in Syria and Iraq.
1251 AD	Hulegu, Manguku's brother, led the Mongol invasion into Persia and established Ilkhanate.

1253 AD	Hulegu's army left from Karakorum and left towards Syria.
1254 AD	Flemish Franciscan friar Wilhelm of Rubruck visited Mangku in Karkorum.
1255 AD	

http://www.scaruffi.com/politics/mongols.html

In the twelfth century, different Turkic and Mongol Tungusic tribes had roamed the steppes of Mongolia. One of the tribes were the Mongols. Around the year 1130, the Mongols had emerged as a very powerful trie, one in which defeated neighbouring nomads and forced the Jin Empire of Northern China to pay tribute. However, the glory was very short lived. In the year 1160, the Mongol Kingdom was then shattered at having been defeated by the Tartars tribe. The Mongol Clans became separate and fought amongst themselves for what little there was left.

Yesugei was the leader of the Mongol Kiyad Sub-Clan, who just happened to be a direct descendant of Khan of the former Mongol Kingdom. In the year 1167, Yesugei and his wife birthed a son by the name of Temujin, the one in which would then become Genghis Khan. When Temujin was only nine years old, his father was poisoned by a chief of the Tartar clan. Since he was too young to rule, the clansmen deserted him. Temujin and his family of seven had moved to the most desolate parts of the steppes. They ate roots and rodents to stay alive. He had many adventures that ranged from chasing horse thieves to being captured by his enemies. When Temujin was only sixteen years old, the Merkid Tribe had attacked his family and had captured his wife. With an army of only five men, Temujin could not retaliate. He turned to one of his father's old friend, Toghrul Khan, which was part of the Kereyid Tribe. He also enlisted a Mongol coalition leader by the name of Jamugha. Together they had defeated the Merkids and rescued Temuin 's wife. Temujin took advantage of the powerful allies, who also happened to be Mongol, as well as childhood friends. They became a notable figure to the steppes. Temujin and Jamugha took over control over most f the Mongol clans. However, that was not enough.

According to the "Secret History of the Yuan Dynasty", one day during which Temujin and Jamugha were riding at the front of Mongols, Temujin had decided to just keep going while Jamugha had stopped to pitch a tent. Temujin broke away from Jamugha and the Mongols were then split into two groups. The hostilities soon then broke out between the two different groups. In clash over the event, Temujin was then defeated and was forced to be exiled. However, Temujin then returned ten years after and reestablished his own position. From there, he had embarked on a conquest of the Mongols that lasted many years. In short, by the year 1204, Temujin had subjugated all that had opposed him. He then defeated the Tartars, the Kereyids, the Naimans, and the Jamugha's Mongol clans.

Empire by the Year 1204

In the year 1206, Temujin held a great assembly on the banks of Onon river. Tere he had taken the title Chingis Khan. The name is commonly referred to as Genghis Khan. However, Genghis is actually a variation, and therefore, for accuracy reasons will be referring to him as Chingis Khan. During the Kjuriltai of the year 1206, Chingis Khan is decreed the structure of the laws for his empire. To ensure that there was stability, as well as cooperation between the tribes, Chingis Khan installed a military superstructure in order to integrate all of the people into his empire. The population was then divided into different units that were responsible for maintaining certain amount of warriors that were ready at any given time. This enabled overriding previous tribal organization. He also decreed many certain law and created an efficient hierarchy for administrative purposes. Chingis Khan created an advanced government and soon proved that his horde was the most disciplined and powerful. He had the most feared army.

War in Northern China

Chingis Khan had become an emperor of those who lived in tents, but his dream was to conquer the entire world. First, he led his army in a series of campaigns against Xi Xia, which was the empire in the western part of China. In the year 1209, the Xi Xia capital was threatened, but the Mongols were all right with the tribute after the camp was unexpectedly flooded. However, as the Empires in China discontinued to pay the tribute once the mongols withdrew, the raids then turned into a conquest.

In the year 1211, Chingis Khan took over 65,000 men and marched against the Jin Empire located in the Northern part of China. With the aid of Ongguts, those people who lived on the northern border, Chingis Khan passed through with ease and marched to Jin territory. He then continued on a trail of plunder until he had met a large force of around 150,000 men, in which he defeated. Chingis Khan split his army up and launched a multiple attacks on Jin. He and the generals dealt many blows against the Jin, which included capturing the strategic Juyong pass. He was wounded during the siege and then withdrew to Mongolia. The Jin forces started to recapture the territories that were lost.

In the year 1213, the Mongols had returned after finding out the Jin had refortified the locations. Chingis then divided his army into three different parts, one was under the command of himself, and the other two was under the control of his sons. The three armies devastated the Jin empire, and by the year 1214, most of the area north was in their hands. One exception was a city of the name Chungdu, which was the capital of the Jin Empire. Like other nomadic type armies, Chingis Khan's hordes were entirely cavalry, and the weakness of the cavalry forces was the lack of skill to capture fortifications. Chingis realized that this weakness and was fast to capture the siege of engineers to learn how to do the siege tactics. Despite so, Chungju withstood the assault. The men became short on supplies and then were ravaged by a plague. However, the Khan tenaciously continued his siege.

First, Move on the West

Khan had lost interest in the war on China and then turned to the west. In the year 1218, he had sent his general Chepe westward and then conquered the Kara Khitai Empire. However, the real issue was the huge Khwarazmian Empire in Persia. Hostilities ended up breaking out when the Khwarazm Shah attacked the Mongol caravan and then humiliated Chingis's ambassadors by burning the men's beards. He was outraged. He prepared for the largest of operations that he had ever performed and assembled a force that was approximately 90,000 to 110,000 men. It was two to three times lesser than the enemy's army; however, Chingis still won due to his leadership. He went on to wage more wars.

Death of Chingis Khan

The campaign that was led against the Xi Xia was the last campaign. Chingis Khan died at the age of sixty years old. The reason that remains unsolved is the differences between the theories of internal injuries after an accident hunting to malaria, even to the prophecies of the Tanguts. At his death, the Empire stretched from the Yellow Sea all the way to the Caspian Sea. No other empire in history had seen such an extraordinary expansion in such a lifetime of just one man. Although Chingis Khan had brought much destruction in his own conquests, it is very clear that he did not intend to commit the mass genocide like that performed by Hitler, even though the tolls of death are far higher than anyone else in history. His dream was conquest, and whenever surrender was seen, then bloodshed was avoided. He was very exceptionally respectful to all those who had supported him, and it was not an uncommon thing for him to befriend defeated enemies. In any case, Khan was a brilliant strategist and was a great and gifted leader. It made him one for most intriguing figures in world history.

Great Khan Ogedei

After the death of Khan, the Mongol Empire was then divided into four different parts that were given to his sons. Although these ulus (the parts of the empire) were politically united in the same empire, that would then later be served as a basis of future khanates. As stated before, Ogedei had already been chosen by Khan to be his successors. Two years later, Ogedei was officially claimed as the ruler of the entire Mongol empire. Ogedei then took the title of Khakhan, which translates to Great Khan. It would be a title that is used by different rulers of the greatest steppe Empires. Khan had never officially used this title, nonetheless, Ogedei ascended with a very smooth transition.

The Mongols won in the war in Russia and pulled off the only successful winter time invasion in Russia's history. As a result, the Mongols swept into Russia, and many groups had fled across the borders and sought out refuge spots located in Hungary. Among these were the Kipchaks and the Cumans, who were also a nomadic cavalrymen just like the Mongols. When Batu Khan had learned of this, he was angered, and due to this, they were not allowed to escape. He found them.

Of course the history goes on and on up until the times of today; however, Khan was the most influential and powerful man throughout history. His legacy lives on through today. This is yet another "rags to riches" story that shows no matter where you come from, no matter who you are, there is always something to conquer to make yourself great.

Conclusion

Thank you again for downloading this book!

With every story comes a past, with every past comes history in which we can learn an extensive amount of knowledge from. From war strategies to the way different cultures lived, you were given much history to digest. This was just covering three major empires, history is something that offers a rich amount of facts and some fiction, but it is up to you, as well as scholars to decipher what is fact and what is myth. There is a theme with these great empires, it includes a person coming up from nothing to conquer territories and men. History throughout shows that one person has the capability to change the world. Will you change history too?

Wait!!!!

If you like this book then feel free to go check out some of this author's other best-selling history books that will keep you on your toes.... CLICK HERE!

Finally, if you enjoyed this book, then I'd like to ask you for a favor, would you be kind enough to leave a review for this book on Amazon? It'd be greatly appreciated!

Click here to leave a review for this book on Amazon!

Thank you and good luck!

Printed in Great Britain
by Amazon